other books by john knoepfle:

rivers into islands, 1965

songs for gail guidry's guitar, 1969

after gray days, 1969

an affair of culture, 1969

john knoepfle

the intricate land

with drawings by

leonel gongora

new rivers press new york 1970

acknowledgements:

the four morticians, morning in the museum, CHICAGO REVIEW;
springfield illinois, FLEUR DE LIS; northwestern moon mask, XAVIER
UNIVERSITY STUDIES; silent day, LAMPETER MUSE; for max jacob who
saw christ in watercolors, REFLECTIONS; in the suburbs, CUMQUAT;
chaff and wheat, AFFAIR OF CULTURE AND OTHER POEMS (Juniper
Books, LaCrosse, Wisconsin, 1969); outpost on the mississippi, COTTONWOOD
REVIEW; in middle kentucky, box score, IOWA STATE LIQUOR STORE;
funeral of christ, CHOICE; noon, THE NATION; state of the union message,
after gray days, AFTER GRAY DAYS AND OTHER POEMS (The Crabtree
Press, Prairie Village, Kansas, 1969); after midnight, TAMBOURINE;
stones, washington nocturne, committee of ways and means, pilgrims day,
grave of jesse james, doing the last things, mary louise, in the late night,
day with an old friend, spring 68, and again spring 68, black hawk questions
the masses, farmer and the owl, heads up another one rising, son of fire,
MINNESOTA REVIEW; national sabbath, LOWER STRUMPFH LAKE
REVIEW; october, trail of tears, AARDWOLF; children, epiphany, ST LOUIS
FREE PRESS; from a missouri land grant, THE MIDWEST MOTORIST.

a number of the poems in this collection were written while time was
available on a grant from the rockefeller foundation

this book was manufactured in the united states for new rivers press,
p.o. box 578, cathedral station, new york, n.y. 10025
in a first edition of 800 copies -

for paul sweeney

who encouraged others
who wanted to write

contents

part one
    red checkers

part two
    golden shadows

part three
  snakes in the rocks

part one

red checkers

springfield illinois

you lose faith today
and tomorrow
a little and by a little
I have come down the valley of the ohio
and I have crossed the state of
illinois in silence
I dont know anymore
what country I am in
here is a restaurant
hamburgers sexy postcards
and I eat
an old dog howls
in the nerves of my teeth

in the late night

the eye
absorbs
the blue picture

detached
from its own
pain bearing
socket

those
who were wounded
are conceived
electronically

now their flesh
returns
to the flesh
of the eye

closing
in the haze
of the living
room

october

we halloween
the real dead with candy
for the sake of the children
the dead who cannot rise
blasted and pumpkined
from the jackolantern smiles
of old folks

groundfog
has closed the airport
at kirksville
fog in the meadows
patches of fog on the highway
all the way north

beeswax ignites
the candied apple
skulls of the living
who hide in a dozen masks
in the corners of their houses
the souls of their faces
bleeding

rain pours in sheets
across the town square
a blonde
witch in her costume
a small unhappy girl
looks up into the rain

mary louise

she knew how the forest was hushed
the animals quiet for three full minutes
before the terrible wind
blew half of the town down

and how benedict arnold
dropped slivers of glass
under the feet of blind beggars
when he was a child

how a group of small boys
laughed at an old man with palsy
and were struck with that trembling
for the rest of their lives

she said we ought to be glad
for hitler and his storm troopers
because no one could ever be more evil
than they were

she kept a long black hatpin
hidden in her spelling book
in case her father or some other man
surprised her in an alley one night

and again spring 68

on this sad evening
I catch a blue moth
and take it
from the candles light

smoke
shambles desire
I think of my children
falling and falling

my gaze
fixes on the light

pilgrims day

mother told the man at the door
you get your ass out of here
and he ran with his chrysanthemum
bobbing upside down in his lapel
we were all amazed
the stuffing we gobbled
hung on our forks in the afternoon
old recollections of providence
at anchor in our blood
until beth my sister with her pansy eyes
said it was truth that our mother
drove away from the door
truth hell cried mother smoothing her skirt
that was your father
and our mouths drooped into oooosss
while we searched the bland face
at the head of the table
then beth with the streaks in her eyes
said who is it carved us the turkey today
truth shouted our mother
now all of you eat
and she clamped her mouth shut on a bun

in middle kentucky

bluegrass boone burley leaf
lovely country
and poor mens houses
falling down on their heads

how you gonna run with these
fine horses jeremiah

poor man couldnt trade
his bourbon gut
for a cedar post

boone didnt want to come back

now they are all boones
black and white boones
running like hell

**winnebago chief
        to the u.s. dragoons
        green bay 1863**

we could not
had we been so disposed
for we have no guns
no ammunition
nor anything to eat
and what is worst of all
one half of our men are dying
from the small-pox

if you will give us guns and ammunition
and pork and flour and feed
and take care of our squaws and children
we will fight you

nevertheless
we will try to fight you
if you want us to
as it is

doing the last things

when the young man is expended
and his eyes are closed
the lashes stilled
like the wings of a moth folded
or fingernails pared
or moons just appearing in an evening darkness
his friends go out and find him
they stretch him out
and cover him perhaps with an old raincoat
walter elias jim do this
for each moment that each one of them will live
though he is dead
it is work that shatters a man
this looking for the friend who is dead
but they move out even under fire
seeking the body

when they carry him to the base camp
the corpsmen preserve him
in an envelop of plastic
and he is sent home
to zanesville or cape girardeau or st paul
wherever it is that was his place
and his unknown family
comes to the lower room in the mortuary
for it is a matter of truth
that is operative now
what has been returned to each family
must be made known again

then the grave is opened
the rifles of the honor guard crack in the morning
and the flag which was spread over the coffin
is folded into a cocked hat
and given to the father or the mother
or his wife the young girl widowed
and the ceremony is finished
later when there is nothing to be gained
the father or the mother or the young girl
receives the sum of three hundred dollars
to the exact farthing
for the cost of the burial

black hawk questions the masses

black hawk sauk warrior
hardnosed type he fought
osage cherokee he fought
the united states badly
lost badly was ball and chained

they took him to washington
gave him the grand tour
all the cities in the east
mobs cheered him in the east

he saw jim crow rice jump jim crow
felt wave on wave baroque
applause saw tears pour down
faces of the audience
sat bemused said why

washington nocturne

the president says shoeshine boy
my kings are invincible
but nobody wants to play checkers anymore
shoeshine boy dont turn the heat down
it may be some drummer
will stop at the white house tonight

the president is old
his face is weathered
like a stone on the north side of a hill
he is sitting in the kitchen
counting his red checker kings
the doorbell is silent
the president is moving a red king
from one square to one other square

now the president removes the kings
takes them from the board and puts them away
he glances around the room absently
he rises and goes to the light cord
and pulls the fierce darkness down
the board is left empty in shadows
not even the moon would look in that place
all that power and the board empty
nothing breathing in the spooky room

shoeshine boy making his rounds
comes to the kitchen in the morning dark
well he says isnt that just like him
hes put the checkers away
and hes left the board out
I wonder who will have at the board next

why maybe I could put some kings on
while nobodys looking I mean but no I dassnt
isnt that a good word dassnt
the old caretaker used it on the boy scouts
when he said he wanted to open the crypt
of william henry harrisons tomb
just to see how the family was holding up
but he dassnt   I think the words better than daunting
that frost used in home burial
but thats just my one opinion
((((shoeshine boy always talked
as if the kiwanis club were listening
sitting around nodding or shaking their heads
he was so well adjusted))))
no sir I would not touch that board
not for the love of all the chinamen on the earth
whoever moves those checkers can destroy the world
but whats that so can I and so can you
you just take a couple of pills
or stab your veins with a penknife
thats how you can destroy the world
and whoever has pretzels and beer in this kitchen
after the old presidents gone will have to know that
um um thats right
but I guess I better go turn the heat down

president padding from the bathroom
holding his teeth in a cup of water
stands at the door and hears shoeshine boy
well he thinks at least when Im out of office
I wont have to put up with him anymore
you get elected by an overwhelming vote
and you have to spend the next four years
listening to a cracker talk about dassant and daunting
and my god william henry harrison
the president swirls the water
around and around the teeth in the cup

george washington wouldnt have dared do that
thats one satisfaction Ive got
he pads off to sleep in his goosefeather bed

well here I am
lafayette park is green in sunshine
dont stare at me
with your eyes bulging eggs
and your mouth
looking like a spoonful of mashed potatoes

youre so serious
you dont like my jokes
cant you see my back is broken
the presidents office is ten stories high
and my wallet is sticky with blood

trail of tears

buried ducks child
passed through hopkinsville
mr reese and myself
remained behind
and buried a child of seabolts
buried rainfrogs daughter
full well I know that many
prayers have gone up
to the king of heaven

national sabbath

men in shadows longer than they are
hold roman candles
lofting their fireballs
red and white
through sycamore trees
and telephone wires
green smoke
drifts over the city

the young man waits
he is alone in the playground

the parade begins
fifes shrill revolutionary airs
men without tongues
men without eyes
men with their kneecaps shot away
they pass in review
they are happy
smiling in the green smoke

the veteran from world war two
raises his candle
he corrects for the wind
a captain of artillery
aiming to the right
of the young mans navel
his aim is rusty
the children shout

whats the matter with our father
but he tells them
have faith my children
and sends the next shot home
the young man glows
a blue wart stung
with an electric needle
and the playground cheers
his burning awhile
for the ohs and ahs of the children
then he vanishes over the city
smiling in the green smoke

words for stones

always at war
even the violets
are raising
their purple faces

four winds over st louis

west wind

a month of straw
burning your lungs
a cotton bowl weeviling
your lungs whining in the
dry maples voices of
presidents the
righteous surety of millionaires
piss of the poor white and chicano
coyotes squashed
on the interstate
purgatorial for the sin of
greed and you damn
all wagons west
and cattle heaving toward abilene
no account cowpokes
flaring blue lightning in their beards
oil heat in a hundred degrees
flaming off the panhandle
cracking the bone gates
of your mothers

south wind

rich mouth treacle air
dripping louisiana booby princess
come alovin you like warm
sweet milk and she like dierdre on her
stone judgment seat
with her toes curled in swamp muck
thumbing down some poor jake
you couldnt tell for black or white
crying see how he looked at me
yall gouge out his eyes and hear
and that one wriggling for my po body
cut off his balls yall
sweet lovely pressing
you down with pussycat stocks and bonds
from plaquemine oh treacherous
mouthing her erous for your
bad lonesome sundowns and you
on parole telling the cop
this starry handled sliver of moonlight
just stuck there in your hand
like shoefly pie
oh you longlegged lean smothering beauty
youd let a man nibble
those perfumed trinkets at your ears
and hang in your noose
halfdead forever

north wind

blue up there and open still
when that cold canada comes glancing
fifes and drums from the arctic
the eye marks fleece in columns
and time withers like an old tit
we get on with new business
everybody has two birds in his hand
you can shrill hozannas
losing your pants
or come free of a steaming earth
with a whistle
and a bellyful of psalms

east wind

plague of frogs
spawned in the chesapeake
boranking boranking
lying cool and plausible in a
slithering death
gagging us like a fungus on the river
saying sall right sall right
where a horn blows in a black
hot night in an empty lot
in east st louis and no angels
answer that horn
splitting the wind

flight to springfield missouri

not so many
flying
the old man
the oldest thing in the sky
heavy smoker
lively and eighty
says we dont think
like they did
the republic
meant something
different to them

we land at leonard wood
the runway
ripped from the hills
like the tongue
from the jaws of a buffalo
the old man
looks out of the window
looks at the edge of the forest
and dreams

poor man to the pulpit

I hear you
like a mouthful
of money

all day
I have been eating
my hands

for max jacob
who saw christ in watercolors

and christ is red rover
he is blazing on the wall in watercolors
and rachel dances in his brain
and her children trail her heels
in flickering pinks and blues

and the armies of the reich
are rising from their graves
they are hiding and seeking
searching and destroying
and the wall is blown down

and christ is reeling in the streets
staining the gutters
with the colors of his blood
and the children are calling
come over come over

silent day

it is a strange day a strange day
even the artichoke has disappeared
there is no sound on the earth
the words of men
have been returned to the void
under the ledges of rock
one jawbone is much like another
all things are serene
from the deep faults of the earth
to the snows on the mountaintops
and we in the dust of our longing
struggle with the ashes of our tongues

tomorrow and today

I walk in my hour
and my hands and my face
are afraid

DRAWINGS FOR

THE INTRICATE LAND

BY LEONEL GONGORA

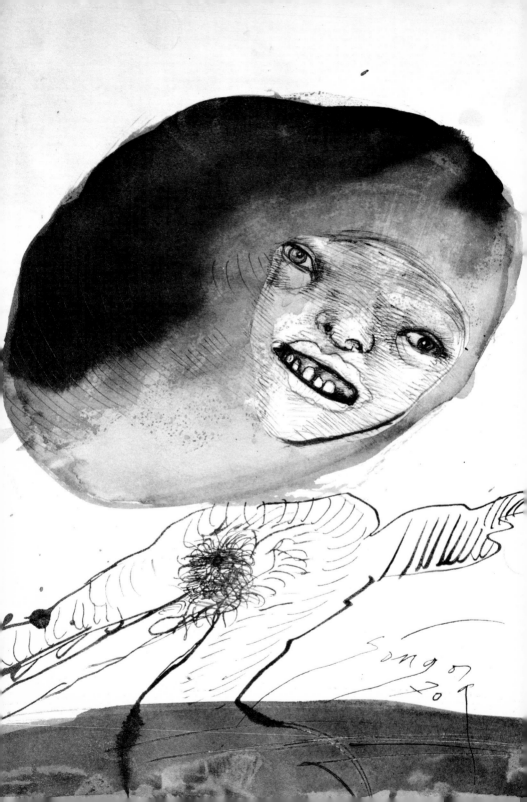

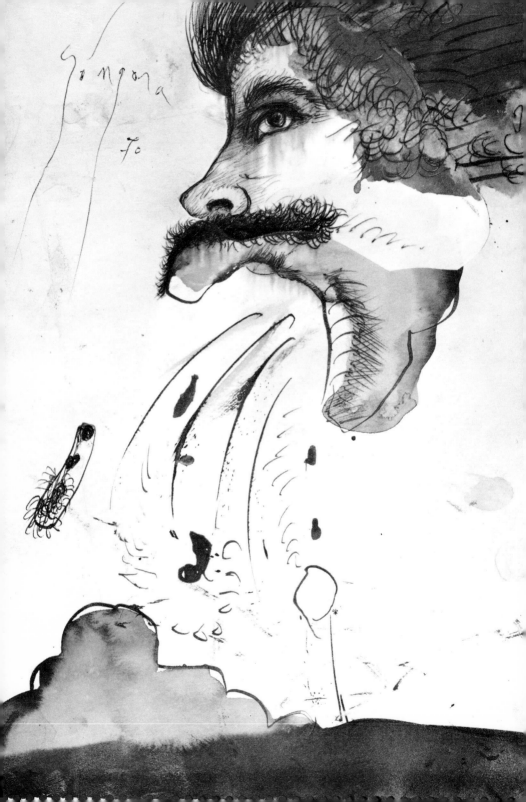

part two

golden shadows

funeral of christ

its that hour   a little string a string
hangs from the neck of christ   it displays
his heart   he has been unpinned   we come
tall men bearing the paneled coffin
the box with the silver initials
mahogany   we carry it up
by its wrought golden handles the crowd
grows heavy in the park around us
a summer storm we raise him up   christ
thrust the body high on our shoulders
and we lurch forward   the crowd
processing behind us and chanting
dies irae oh dies irae
as the clergy censes the evening
one hundred thousand red monsignors
it is an orderly procession
acolytes with portable bullhorns
harry the stragglers   when indians
join us at the citys edge singing
carne vale carne vale sad
among the great whites and negroes move
through the crowd grief splintering their bones
we think we are companionable
members of the press work like lean dogs
they wrench at one anothers shoulders
vying for camera positions
they take a thousand pictures thrashing
among bloodstained palms   a thousand six
for a special blacklined supplement
no one smiles not one man smiles for them
we carry christ through the potters field

and across the lawns of the cemetary
green landscapes of the cemetary
there is no space among the graveplots
we trample down the stones we knock down
the headstones   miller goes down and knapp
mcavoy and cargas and benoit
montesi go down   we find his grave
opened before we carried him here
the coffin is lowered   the golden
handled roses are dropped down   lilies
his silver initials are covered
with forgetmenots   we sing to him
farewell sweet flesh of christ farewell now
we do not know in our houses now
who died or who will come and walk earth

the four morticians

he drinks some very hot coffee
with four sympathetic morticians

they have come from the rain
the smell of pitch in the burning magnolia

they ask him why he would leave
his children wife child shocked in her womb

he answers someone wanted me
I joined another man and became him

too bad too bad they tell him
the man you were was surely not happy

but I tell you I looked from his eyes
and suddenly we shouted with joy

we will have to be sorry for you
considering the arrangements meanwhile

they study their four mugs of coffee
smiling with four easy smiles

we can make you serenely contented
or express you with pious hope

I would never have been so ambitious
just dont let my mouth drop down

well we can trammel your jawbone
with our secret and adequate wires

thank god for the wires and my forehead
the crease there let it remain

it is not very professional
but we will consent to leave it unwaxed

the four morticians stand up
they take him by the shoulders and the knees

the wisest of the morticians smiles
your joy you know it could not have lasted

oh I suppose you have to be right
but what of you with nothing but death to live for

we must go the office   girls will be coming
longing for pecan rolls and their coffee

noon

we have the power now
we administer   our
progenitors are dead we talk
angrily thinking of the young

this is the time when enemies
are known to us and when our friends
call us up on the phone
and they say we need you now

oh yeah

we was in the nicest country
everybody gave us watermelons

bus station

kansas city
waiting for the bus
bus going to lawrence
whites the
country people
smiling their teeth
rotten children
weak in the chest asthmatic
blacks looking
healthy
sickness hiding
ulcerous in the gut
well neighbors
enemies
how about some advice
good advice
where is the next
bus to lawrence
coming from

committee of ways and means

it is the custom now
the great voices
of the world speak out

give them something to eat
because they are hungry
and the mountains
will fall down with joy

everywhere hands
applaud
everywhere
a crying of birds
a great migration

all the darkness
of the world applauding

hands applauding
hands opening and closing
hands rising and falling

assemblies of hands
congresses of hands
applauding applauding

grave of jesse james

here comes old mother
she greets visitors to the farm
charges them each a quarter
they go look at the grave
she charges them each a quarter
for pebbles they want to take home
it is a miraculous grave
it multiplies stones overnight
small round creekworn pebbles
squeezing up from the earth
helping to support mother
mother is tough
sitting in the yard in her sunbonnet
rocking the old sun down

in the suburbs

the man runs down our street
his face is a golden fire
he calls out give me your coins
the eyes of the dead
have need of our money
give me your coins
and I will cover
the eyes of the dead

box score

the prophet
drinks beer
from a can
he pulls the tab
and when he is through
bends the can
inside his fist
a feat of strength
for the younger men

he doesnt
have anything to say
what is there left
to say

he goes
to the ballgame
watches steve carlton
set a new
strike out record

he wonders
what did they die of
in the old days

he has it
in his mind
his word
will be the last

long summer

the exhortations
the appeals
the shoutings
the cursings
I believe the sergeant in the bunker
saying gee whiz

state of the union message

fellow americans
white water lilies drop roots into muck
if we stop this muck
we will kill our water lilies

count down on the moon

then the astronauts
came to the head of the holler
where the blind child
was playing with her cat
she lived in a cabin
with nothing in it
and there was nothing in the holler
except four oil wells
they said missy you have been selected
we have come to take your eyes to the moon
and she said land sakes you can have my eyes
if you bring my daddy a bigger
welfare check but they said missy
that is another department
and she had to give up her eyes anyway

they took them to the launching pad
took them in a plastic box
they all went up in a rocket
and we all watched on television
that rocket go up to the moon

the child said to her cat
who was siamese
and had great blue eyes like a grizzly bear
I think its a bad thing uncle
to die in the dark
she said uncle you remember
saint catherine of siena
said to the pope why old man
its good to be pope
but its better to look like a pope
well uncle thats what it is with me

a week ago I looked like a child
shining in light and now
I dont know

she was pretty
she had a shock of black hair
and a heartshaped face
and where her eyes were
it was like kettles
inverted copper kettles
or small teacups painted green
a girl could play with
on a morning that was lonesome

the astronauts were long in orbit
over the earth and yawing in space
observed by a smother of stars
when the blind childs eyes slipped from their box
and stood in midair peering at them
and they said hey and oh what the heck
get those damn eyes back in the box
but those eyes like a careful woman
would not be taken when they were not ready
and the astronauts began itching in their suits
feeling little in their cribs
with their mothers bending over
staring at them

so they called houston houston
what will be do about these eyes
and a baldheaded professor from cincinnati said
when I count three pollute your capsule
and they all yelled hurray and okiefenokie
and filled their capsule with everything
with garters pins needles cookey crumbs shoelaces

peanut shells parts of transisters
graham crackers hot dogs party favors
until the eyes were fouled in the litter
and they felt better
and went to sleep for eight hours

the child said
uncle I am so sad
I am like a country song
everything sad in me is real
but if I tried to smile or play
ring around the rosie
I would be a banjo picker
down there in nashville
making a sly face
and rolling my eyes in my head
and they wouldnt let me go on television

then they landed on the moon
went out in their wonderful space suits
elephants huge in their satins
ponderously leaping and laughing
like a high school football team
goosed by the principals daughter
churchbells rang through the nation
the president made a long distance phone call
the child said
I think it is time uncle
tell my daddy I think it is time
and the astronauts
buried her eyes on the moon
and she died in the holler
when her blind eyes died on the moon

they came back home to the earth
they were sad
and everybody was sad
everybody dug a small grave
on the hillside under a cypress
and they left the child there
at the moons rising
and then the strange light
searched the holler
touching the cabin the oil wells
the cypress and the grave
longing for something it had known
hidden in a darkness there

uncle came from the cabin
we walked in the moonlight
and sat on the grave
he looked at the world with his big blue eyes
and he didnt do anything

morning in the museum

now observe in this painting
  boy be quiet
the christ of the antillas
the silver antillas
a marvelous depiction
clothed in the scales of a fish
and crowned with bananas
his eyes are the skins
the golden skins of bananas
his nose is a long banana
and between his legs
  boy please be quiet
another peeled beautiful banana
he is nailed to that tree
with four additional bananas
his fingers are sprouting
some very small green bananas
his mouth is stuffed with bananas
the soldiers are stuffing
his mouth with bananas
  boy why did you spit
  on this wonderful picture
this christ of the antillas
king of bananas
this golden shadow
swimming the silver antillas

chaff and wheat

my words drone
serious preacher
the blacksnake sleeps
on my wishbone

part three

snakes in the rocks

after gray days

nobody knows
what to do

you take pills
get the word from television
eat right food
you wander around an afternoon

when its raining
your blood wants you to whittle
but that isnt done now

then seomone comes up on the porch
with his hair beading water
and rain dripping off his nose

he says that the chinese
think of america
as that far country
of a thousand flowers

you smile at him suddenly
you think if you could only
release maybe fifty million balloons
over asia saying good luck to you chin
from the land of a thousand flowers
some golden years
might pour down time

you peer through store windows
watching the shoplifters
you think why are we all
thieves in our bandages

and the snakes in the rocks hissing
come crush our heads
flay us hang our long skins
on the screen doors of your houses

after midnight

now your hair is deep water
and the moonlight shoals
the hollows of our face
and I dream here in myself

should I wake you
my lovely country

should I tell you I know
that when a man
surveys his possessions
the promontory is lonely

day with an old friend

tom drives and we come
through the negro now of this
old neighborhood
where my parents are rested
beneath a young oak
a prospect named calvary
as I remember

we are not young men anymore
toms hair grays his face
and my father is dead these twenty years
my mother ten
I cannot believe
the numbers carved on the stones
but I am contented seeing how the oak leaves
curl around their names
and there is a little wind
alert on his blue day

it has been four years this time
I cannot think what to do
tom says the single prayer

we go back to the car
he would like to show me his horses
he tells me of the city
drawn bloodless with the fear
of a mad strangler on the loose
a city filled with murderous thoughts

that evening I drive it alone
over the new bridge into kentucky

outpost on the mississippi

the french commander
addressed the indian villagers
he was about four feet five
he told them I have a little body
but my heart is big enough
for everyone
the indians believed him

they are all gone into time now
the commander
the french soldiers
the indians

the afternoon is hazy
tourists wander the park
a family walks a balance
on the stone foundation
of the commissary
a man and a woman
blow alternately
on their picnic fire
the planet is rolling slowly
to accommodate the scene

he says do you believe me
I say the whole nation
wants to believe you

children

outside my window
I hear my children
bickering in the yard
sparrows of the race
contentious who cannot provide
innocent because
they have no foresight
owls of my own darkness

heads up another one rising

here is another one
ready to celebrate all hallows eve
an anonymous old man
who starved in st louis
a long time ago
perhaps a slave in a limestone cell
or an irish roustabout on the landing
he is restive in his box
heart beating rudely in the black
cavern under his ribs
his white old skull grinning
as of course they all do
from the shudder of the heart
that sets the bones vibrating
he is stirred up all right
his tubular arms extending
pushing out the lid of the coffin
against the st louis sundown
sun going down like that same old man
descending into a steam bath once
and now his wristbones
force the cover back on the evening
stars slide down the lid
as his universe expands
they go down as he comes up

farmer and the owl

farmer said to this owl he caught
okay you skinny prophet
lets see how you light up the dark
theres your tailfeathers
diddled in kerosene
and struck to hells fire with my match
owl fussed and flared in the yard
screeched hoo hoo   hoo hoo hoo
o god of all owls
stiffen my bones with manganese
and you you son of a kansas fathead
bawl out loud when you see my revelations
here I go and haylofts to the last of me
o my virginal owlsoul
may you rise with a pure blue flame
from the ashes of this barn tonight
farmer watched his barn burn down
birdshit   he said birdshit
dirty pious birdshit   birdshit

northwestern moon mask

whoever carved this face
did it to please his chief
who was arrogant
nothing left of him now
but this mask

the chief burned his goods
his copper beads boats his slaves too
thinking to shame a rival prince
when that devil
could sneer enough wealth
to mock despair

did the maker hide his mask

warriors took their chief away
with his charred head lolling
when he threw himself on the fire
his rival tossing off copper
like so much rain

but do not judge him
things killed this chief
and he killed himself

he did not understand his mask
speaking to him of want
which she alone supplied
and coming in a darkness
flowing with content
to fill what she had no need to fill

son of fire

in that beginning
the grand captive of horizons
slid down his eucalyptus tree
and adored an old water buffalo
he had been studying for years and years
with more care than his wifes own
speckled behind up in the high perch
because he determined
there was nothing living among flowers
that could measure his friendly eyes
and so he made gods
of all things that moved in the world
and wore a small raisin
stitched to a thong on his neck
with a singular cunning

spider

avatar

crabby
image of myself

dont you know
that even I

can change

**for lucien vic norman
john frieda rocco frank linda
walter ann kelly jett ted
elaine al ed leola and joe**

I write
of our days
of springs
of caves
of places
we have come from
of a quarter turn
another season
of us in our names
with our chance
at joy
of waters
under earth
of flowers
in the mountains
melting
through snow

from a missouri land grant

ozark spring

blue coin of earth generous in all that
green hickory light shafting
through elm and the smell of cedars
clinging and faint in a
rocky soil
under old mountains
hills worn down with so many seas

water
swelling from the cliffbase
blue deep blue silky
flowing
shallow over pebbles
a clear channel
light green
dark green
cress bannering
tan stones and dots of small
black snails grown used to the sheer
chill of the stream

quiet too with lily and the lotus
and back in the deep hole of the spring
place of half visible rock
shelving the eye down to deeper blue
trout hanging indolent
sustained there
beyond our beginnings

shut ins

east fork
through the ridged porphyry
cutting the igneous stone
purple and polished on the spurs
of the side trail
narrow over the river
we climb down
working through rapids
the wet rock slippery
small falls catching us
helpless into pools
laughing
though you sense
deep openings in crevices and
terror a little
it is easier
at the foot of high gray cliffs
a larger pool slowing green water
where you can dive or leap
thirtyfive feet from
steep ledges or
watch others do that
and sicken with the thudding
the body makes
hurled onto a surface
you tense when a boy dives
waiting his shot upward
from surges of white foam
face all smiles for the
manhood in it
lazy then you climb up current
goatfooting cracked boulders
and choose one to rest on
shut in the sunlight
and grateful

we picnic in a grove
shady with cedar
the ground in park grass
and flinty at the gullies
I find a knife
blue chert chipped
with so much care
a meticulous hand
and then a cruder point
old and shaped lanceolate
from seven thousand years
a hunters work who knew
the continent in gales of dust
come here with his women
his kinsmen maybe
everyone to climb rocks and falls
all watching one another
solemn birds or sleepy animals
or flashing white teeth
in brown human faces
with a sparkle of water
shimmering tits and thighs
for the joy of it
life so short then
before the women were spent
and the pain of that
arthritic wilderness
crippled those hunting hands
he must have
loved this place

granite

lower ranges
stones heavy
at the edge of the valley
grinders for rending
time into powders
we cross pile on pile
of the red stone squeezing through
deceived the stones
looming larger as we come
west to the edge
place of stunted oak
and dry scale on the stones
like copper weathered
nothing moves
seems to have ever moved
even the names of the quarrymen
appear to be chiseled forever
fingers and the palm of your hand
rough out the bolders
pitted and windswept
scarred by ancient waters
and the heart forgets the rhythm
of its own beating
and the body
comes to its own coil in the rock
for awhile
and then you go back
stone underfoot
scattering into dust
a littered trail
and the vision dies in a
gleam of chrome and cars
you notice it is a hot day
and time has you again
but not quite again

fisher cave

caving going
down into the earth
cool there with our
jonah shadows apprehensive
seeing what has been hidden
waiting for our coming
lanterns filling chambers
riches of onyx and clay
for the potters wheel
broken splendors
and our messages
whatever we carry for someone
who will listen to us
if he hears us

where have we come from
the hot day all
our lives to this station
subdued in corridors
the lost rivers of the world
have etched under the earth

we return
wearing our chill like a sleeve
the air hazing
at the caves mouth
and come to ourselves again
not knowing to what purpose
kings throwing dust in their hair
our sulking perhaps
under vines in the
punishing sun

salt lick

it is sullen here
the mud flat
will not bear life
where the saline springs
flecked with silver
widen into rivers
that will absorb them

boone made this spring box
I look into the waters
shaped with his hands
and stare with his eyes
at the suppressed
continents of the earth

the mud captures each leaf
the prints of the raccoons
seem held now for years
that will number in the thousands

for the marriage
of john and paula ashton

in places that are known
to be dangerous
the lovers
move with their cares
wanting their survival
desiring with their bodies
with the spirits
of their children

they go on to the mountain
to the worn ridges
to places where men were
that are abandoned
they discover the old caves
the hearths with the stones
broken and they kindle
their new fires

camped in our valleys
we look up from our own
evening fires
and see the hilltops burning
the flames of the lovers
find us
and we grow peaceful
wondering

epiphany

herod is eating out tonight
he is dining on the head of
john the baptist

jesus blessing little children
thinks of his good friend john

audie pokes at a rock
with her magic stick
irridescent beetles
fumble in the grass

audie audie what are they
angels angels
taking over the world

days becoming older

the gold fox
stands
at my side
the fox has a dripping
tongue